Japanese Etiq

The Complete Guide to Japanese
Traditions, Customs, and Etiquette

DINGO
B O O K   C L U B

"Great Books Change Life"

Table of Contents

Introduction

The Japanese people have an extensive range of customs, rituals, and forms of etiquette for all aspects of their lives. These forms of etiquette are not only interesting for non-Japanese but also open our eyes to the fact that despite the huge strides Japan has made in terms of modern-day advancement in technologies, the age-old customs and traditions are still a deeply-embedded part of their society.

They revere and respect their customs, traditions, and other forms of etiquette and expect people visiting from other countries to do so too. Similarly, the Japanese people are equally respectful of other people's traditions, customs, and etiquette and work hard to understand them so that they don't make a mistake when they visit other countries.

In fact, if you were to travel with any of the Japanese tourist organizations to other countries, the first thing that the guide will talk about is the etiquette expected to be followed there. The Japanese believe that they are ambassadors of their nation and they have to work hard to ensure they leave behind a good impression of their country and its people.

Taking a page out of their etiquette book, it makes a lot of sense to learn about the Japanese forms of etiquette so that we can be prepared to do the right thing at the right time in the right place when we travel to Japan. Moreover, knowing about the culture of another country is a fabulous way of opening our minds and celebrating world differences.

Minding your behavior and your manners reflects a deep sense of discipline and respect for the society and the people you are interacting with. Taking this one step further, the Japanese are a wee bit more attached to etiquette and good behavior than many other countries in the world. As stated earlier, behind the façade of modernity, Japan still is ruled and governed by age-old customs and traditions that are taken very seriously.

The most obvious aspect of these customs and traditions is the etiquette that is unique to Japan and its people. Despite the vast changes in the political, economic and social realms that the country has witnessed over the past hundred years, it has retained its etiquette repertoire in all its ancient splendor and glory.

The modern Japanese take pride in following their forefathers' footsteps in the art of good behavior and pass on their learning to their children too in an effort to keep the traditions alive for many more centuries to come.

This book is written with the intention of giving you insights into the various forms of etiquette the Japanese followed in different social and business settings. Ranging from the correct usage of names and greetings right up to wedding and funeral customs, as much information as possible has been included in this book.

With the etiquette tips in this book, you will be able to handle the expectations of the courteous and polite people of Japan in terms of good behaviour and manners. Most of the people are happy to welcome guests and tourists with open arms and will be even more obliged to do their best to make your stay in their country happy and worthwhile if you show an effort to replicate their etiquette norms and requirements.

Chapter 1: The Use of Names

One of the most important elements of Japanese etiquette is to be aware of how to address people and how to use names in different social and business settings.

Addressing People with Respect

San is a commonly used respectful expression that is put at the end of people's names while addressing them. San can be used when using the first name or the last name of the concerned individual. Also, san is used for all people irrespective of marital status or gender.

Sama is a term that is more appropriate in a formal setting and is to be used after the family name. Also, you must remember that you must use san or sama after everyone else's name (whom you wish to show respect to) but not after your own name. Here are some examples of the use of san and sama:

- Smith-san (Mr. Smith)
- Michael-san (Mr. Michael)
- Sandra-san (Ms. Sandra)
- Smith-sama (Mr. Smith again but to be used in a formal setting only)
- Tanaka-sama (Ms. Tanaka)

Another way of respectful address is by using the job title of the person along with his or her name. This works in a scenario where you need to address your superior at work or your teacher at school. For example, you can say Brown-sensei

(Brown teacher; sensei is teacher in Japanese) instead of saying Brown-sama. Or bucho-san which is referring to your department head; bucho is head in Japanese.

In business environments, using surname instead of given or first name is more respectful. Use of one's job title instead of their name is also well accepted in Japanese business circles. This subtlety of using surnames instead of first names might come across as a bit stiff for some non-Japanese. However, you must remember that most Japanese are uncomfortable using first names.

However, there are a few Japanese citizens with a lot of exposure to Western cultures that have come to accept being addressed by their first names. Some of them have taken this even further and have created nicknames for themselves, which they embrace happily. You can use these nicknames too along with san or sama depending on the level of formality of the setting.

The final tip here is to remember that you can never go wrong using the surname with the san or sama suffix. For all else, it would be prudent to ask around and then make a sensible choice of addressing the concerned person. The convenience of san cannot be underestimated considering that it is unisex and, therefore, you don't have to worry about how to address people through email especially if the Japanese names are not clearly gender-specific.

Also, if someone is addressing you with the san suffix, accept it as a compliment. That's the intention of the Japanese name-calling etiquette.

Addressing Family and Friends

In Japan, addressing family members and friends also calls for politeness and respect though there is less formality than the use of san or sama. There is a plain form and there is a polite form when it comes to addressing family and friends. Here are a few examples:

- Otto or goshujin – husband
- Tsuma or okusan - wife
- Okoson – child in a polite form and Kodomo – child in a plain form
- Otosan – father in a polite form and Chichi – father in a plain form
- Okāsan – mother in a polite form and haha – mother in a plain form
- musukosan – son in a polite form and musuko – son in a plain form
- musumesan – daughter in a polite form and musume – daughter in a plain form
- otōtosan – older brother in a polite form and ani – older brother in a plain form
- onēsan – older sister in a polite form and ane – older sister in a plain form
- imōtosa – younger sister in a polite form and imōto – younger sister in a plain form
- tomodachi – friend

During conversations, shujin is used to refer to one's own husband and otto is used to refer to someone else's husband. Tsuma is used to refer to one's own wife and kanai is used to refer to someone else's wife

Here's the trick when it comes to using the plain form or the polite form. If you are addressing an older member of the family, then you must use the polite form. When addressing the younger members of the family (spouse also comes in the category), you can use the plain form. To get this right, you must also know the difference between referring to someone and addressing someone.

Referring to someone means you are not talking to the person but are referring to him or her in a conversation with someone else. Addressing someone, on the other hand, is talking to the person directly.

Commonly Used Japanese Expressions

While we are at this, let me also give you the top five commonly used expressions in Japanese conversations:

Yatta – I did it! – You can use this term whenever you have accomplished or been offered a great job or have won something. All these occasions can be classified under the 'Yatta' category.

Honto – Really? – This expression is used to let the person speaking to you know that you are listening to what is being said.

Â, SÔ DESU KA – I see – Also, a conversational bit of phraseology letting your partner (the one who is talking to you) know you are getting what is being said. A nod invariably accompanies this expression.

Mochiron – of course! – An expression of confidence

Zenzen – not at all – a phrase of emphatic denial (in a polite way) used for situations such as when someone asks you, "Am I disturbing you?" and you politely say, "zenzen."

Chapter 2: Greetings and Body Language Etiquette

There are many ways of greeting people when you meet them. This chapter is dedicated to these Japanese greeting methods.

Bowing

Bowing, or bending at the waist level, is a form of appreciation and respect shown by the person who is bowing to the person who is being bowed to. Bowing is a common form of greeting used along with:

- Good morning - ohayo gozaimasu
- Hello, good afternoon - konnichi wa
- With words of apology or gratitude (arigato)

There are three types of bows depending on how deep the waist is bent. These three types include:

The casual bow (eshaku bow)

Bending at a 15-degree angle, the casual bow also entails a slight tipping of the head. The eshaku bow is used when casual greetings are passed between people or when you pass someone belonging to a higher social status. Casual greetings in the form of good morning or good afternoon or thank you are sufficient by themselves. Yet, when used along with the eshaku bow makes the greeting more heartfelt.

The business bow (keirei bow)

This bow entails bending your torso at 30 degrees and is used when entering and/or leaving a meeting or conference or while greeting customers.

Deep bow (saikeirei bow)

This is the politest form of bowing in Japan and entails lowering the torso by 45 degrees. It is used to express very deep feelings of regret (apology) or gratitude.

Clasping Hands (Gassho)

Bringing both the palms together and clasping them in front of the chest is referred to as gassho. This form of greeting has its origins in Buddhism. Today, it is used before starting a meal and after finishing the meal along with the word, 'itadakimasu.' The word, 'itadakimasu,' means to receive or to accept an item or gift. It expresses gratitude for the food and for the person(s) who prepared the meal.

Bye-Bye

While 'sayonara' is the Japanese word for saying goodbye, the phrase 'bye-bye;' is also commonly used in the country. There is a subtle difference in the way the hand gesture works with sayonara. While in the West, you would open and close your palm as you lift your hand, in Japan, your open palms are waved from left to right and back. The hand is lifted high above your head so that the other person can see it and then the open palms are waved from left to right and back in a broad arch. The eshaku bow is also used commonly while saying bye-bye.

Shaking Hands

Although bowing is the more appropriate Japanese form of greeting, the handshake has come to be an accepted form of greeting, especially in a business setting. However, it is important to note that the handshake of the Japanese is far limper than the 'firm handshake' of the Western culture. This is easy to understand considering that the Japanese culture does not allow for too much physical contact, especially in public.

Body Language Etiquette

Nodding is an important gesture in Japan. When you arc talking to someone, it is important that you nod often to imply comprehension. Your nod is telling the speaker that you are listening to him or her, and you are understanding what the person is trying to say.

Silence is an accepted form of nonverbal communication. There is no need to chatter merely to keep a conversation going. Silence is, in fact, an expected means of communication. Talk only when addressed or when it is your turn to do so.

Standing very close to a Japanese person is considered rude and uncomfortable. Avoid touching as much as possible except for that first handshake (the bow is a better option).

Making prolonged eye contact when talking to someone is also considered rude in Japanese culture.

Hugging, shoulder slapping, and other forms of physical contact are also to be avoided, especially in public. The Japanese frown on any outward show of affection of any kind.

Using your forefinger to beckon is disallowed. The Japanese way of beckoning calls for extending your right arm and bending the wrist in the downward direction. You are not allowed to beckon any person older than or senior to you.

How to Sit Correctly

Sitting in Japanese style calls for sitting on the floor and in an upright position. Even meals are had while sitting on the floor with low tables for the food. For tea ceremonies, it is mandatory to sit on the floor.

Both genders use the kneeling, or the seiza, posture to sit in a formal environment. It can get uncomfortable after some time for people (especially Westerners) who are not used to this way of sitting. In modern times, foreigners are exempted from sitting on the floor. In fact, many modern Japanese also find it difficult to sit like this for long. In casual environments, it is common to see men sitting cross-legged and women sitting with both their legs to one side.

If you are sitting on a chair, you are expected to sit with both your feet firmly placed on the ground. You cannot cross your legs or place your ankle on the knee while sitting on the chair.

The seating order works something like this: the most important person (usually the customer or the guest) is furthest away from the door. The place that is farthest away from the door is considered to be the good side in Japanese culture.

If there is a tokonoma (an alcove decorated with a hanging scroll accompanied by a flower arrangement), then the guest is usually placed in front of it. The least important person or the host takes the place closest to the door.

Also, in a business environment, all the people from the same company are seated on the same side of the table. When you visit Japanese businesses, it is common for the receptionist to show you your seat. If you don't see this happening, it might be prudent to ask before taking a seat.

Chapter 3: Bathing Etiquette (Onsen)

Bathing has two connotations in Japanese culture. While one meaning is what non-Japanese people are most familiar with is to cleanse the body, the second connotation is to use bathing as a means of relaxation. Bathing for the second reason is a great cultural experience in Japan. Initially, you might feel intimidated and, perhaps, even a bit shy. But once you get used to the joys of the Japanese bathing experience, it can become an addiction.

Like all things in Japan, using the public baths (for relaxation purposes) is replete with behaviours of etiquette everyone is expected to follow. The baths, or onsens, dot the entire landscape of the country and you will find many as you travel through Japan. Not following bathing etiquette is deeply frowned upon. So, here are the etiquette steps you should be aware of:

Entrance to the Baths

The entrances to most of the baths are covered with 'noren' curtains that act like fabric dividers for privacy. There are separate baths for men and women. Women get the blue noren and the men get the red noren.

It is important that you check for the right bath before entering. Quite often, the baths are switched which means what was the women's in the morning could become men's in the evening and vice versa. So, please check carefully and ensure you open the right noren.

Changing Rooms

These rooms are attached to the onsens and are usually equipped with locker facilities and/or baskets for your clothes. There are some onsens that also have hair dryers, chairs, and other facilities here. It is important to check if the onsen you are visiting has toilet facilities or else you must visit the toilet before entering the bath.

The changing room is where you will take off all your clothes and put them in your designated basket or locker. Valuables, jewelry, accessories and spectacles should also be removed and placed here. Slippers are not usually allowed inside onsens. There will be a place outside earmarked for footwear.

Washrooms

Washrooms are different from the relaxing bathing areas (in the form of tubs or hot springs). You must first cleanse your body in the washroom. Rinse yourself thoroughly to ensure no oil, shampoo, or soap is still lingering on your body. Only then; can you step into the bath. The bathing area is only for soaking and relaxing.

The following steps will help you through the process of bathing in Japanese onsens while ensuring no breach of etiquette occurs:

- Clothes have to be removed in the changing rooms
- Cleanse, rinse, and wash your body
- Get into the bath and soak and enjoy yourself

Tips for Bathing Etiquette

Before

Follow the red and blue noren curtains and ensure you enter the bath meant for your gender. Visit the toilet before you get inside the bath. Drink sufficient water to prevent the risk of dehydration.

Remove clothes, valuables, and other accessories in the changing room and place in your designated locker/basket. Cleanse and rinse your body in the washing rooms. Tie up your hair if it is very long. A modesty towel is usually supplied to cover yourself when you move between the bathing area and the washing area. Excessive intake of food and alcohol should be avoided before the bathing ritual.

During

Use of the modesty towels also has etiquette to follow. Men cover their private parts with them, and the women cover themselves from the breasts downward to the genitals. As soon as they enter the bath, the towels are moved up to cover their heads. When they come out of the bath, the towels from the head position move to the prvious position again.

As the areas surrounding the bath will be wet and slippery, it is essential that you walk carefully. Rinsing and washing your body is not allowed in the bathing area. It is restricted to the washing areas only. There are options where you can do a quick rinse using the water from the bath. However, you can do this only by dipping some water into a washing bowl and then slowly rinse and cleanse yourself OUTSIDE the bath and not inside. Only when you are clean can you enter the bath.

Some onsens may not have showers in the washroom. In such places, buckets will be provided. If there is no separate supply of water for the washrooms, you can dip the bucket (or wash bowl) and fill it with water from the tub itself. Some places have stools with water faucets you can use to cleanse yourself. Please check if the facility you are visiting supplies soap and towels or else you might have to carry your own. Remember to return the wash bowl/bucket back to where you took it from so that others can use it.

Do not put your towel, soap, shampoo, or anything else inside the tub. Ensure your towel is on your head or near the side of the bath. You are free to get in and out of the bath any number of times as you wish. Most of the places do not allow for wearing swimming suits. No smoking or washing clothes in the wash area.

After

 Don't forget to retrieve your valuables and other items from the changing rooms. Drinking something after your soak is good for rehydration. Some onsens have massaging and relaxing rooms where bathers sit or sleep and relax after the soak. Wet towels should not be placed on the floors. Put them in the designated place.

Some More Important Tips

- Tattooed people are not allowed in some onsens. Please check before you go.
- Menstruating women or infants are not allowed in onsens.

While these are some of the basic etiquette tips for bathing in Japan, once you get used to them, you will find it great to visit onsens as often as you can because they are truly relaxing.

Chapter 4: Restaurant and Dining Etiquette

Whether you are having a business dinner in Japan, or eating at someone's home, or simply having dinner with Japanese friends, dining and restaurant etiquette plays a crucial role to ensure you are doing what the Japanese people expect you to. Here are some tips on restaurant and dining etiquette.

Sitting arrangements

A typical Japanese meal happens on low tables with diners sitting on cushions next to the tables. The seating cushions are placed on the tatami (a mat made with a reed-like element) floor close to the low tables. If the dinner is a formal one, then both the men and women kneel (seiza posture). In an informal atmosphere, the men sit cross-legged while the women have both their legs on one side.

The seat of honor

This is especially followed in a formal setting where the guest of honor (or the most important person in that group) is seated on the kamiza, or the seat of honor. The kamiza is always the farthest away from the entrance.

Towels (or the Oshibori)

In most bars and restaurants, before the beginning of the meal, hot steamed towels known as the oshibori are given to each diner. This towel is for cleaning your hands only. You are not allowed to wipe your face with it. In a home setting, the guests are requested to wash their hands before sitting down to the meal.

Eating

In a restaurant, after everyone has ordered, it is common practice to wait until everyone's order is served before eating. The meal is started after the waitress (in a restaurant), family member (at home) or the guest of honor (in a formal setting) gives the signal to begin eating. The process of eating is usually started by saying the word, 'itadakimasu' which translates to 'I gratefully receive.'

If you are eating from small-sized individual bowls, then you must lift the bowl close to your mouth and eat from it. However, this should not be done with the larger bowls containing dishes that everyone at the table will take from.

When serving yourself from bowls or common dishes, then you must either use the non-eating end of the chopsticks or use the set that is kept specifically for serving.

Burping, blowing noses, or any kind of loud munching sounds made at the dining table are frowned down upon by the Japanese people. A classic example of Japanese good eating manners clearing your plate/bowl right down to the last grain of rice.

Food should be ideally eaten in one bite. Therefore, you can be prepared to earn some frowns from the guests at the table if you bite your food into smaller pieces. Food should also not be raised above the level of your mouth.

A special note on soup consumption in Japan: Japanese soups contain a lot of ingredients and therefore a spoon is not suitable for it. The ideal way is to slurp up the liquid and use chopsticks to eat the solid ingredients. Yes, you heard right, you don't have to worry about slurping soup in Japan. Inhaling air as you eat the noodles in the soup is supposed to enhance the taste.

Japanese Miso soup

A special note for sushi: Wasabi ideally should not be added to soya sauce for your sushi dip. The sushi pieces that combine well with wasabi already contain it. If you add wasabi into your sushi dip, then you are, in effect, offending the chef, which is not allowed.

Japanese Sushi set

Chopsticks

The correct use of chopsticks is one of the primary elements of dining etiquette in Japanese culture. The chopsticks have to be held in the correct way. You must never put the chopsticks standing upright on any dish because this is done only during funeral rituals. You must never directly eat from a common dish. You must serve yourself in a smaller bowl and eat from there. You should also remember not to hover your chopsticks over a dish as you think about what you want to eat.

When you are not using the chopsticks, then you must place them on the dedicated stand (called hashioki) meant for this or simply put them down. It is considered impolite to talk to people at the table while holding the chopsticks in your hand. You should not use chopsticks as a pointer and you must never use your chopsticks to pass on food to someone else. Use the wrong end of the chopsticks to serve or use the set that is kept specifically for serving.

Drinking

'Kampai' is the drinking salute in Japan. You must wait until everyone has a drink of front of them and then a salute is called before you can start drinking. It is absolutely essential that you do not pour your own drink. In Japanese culture, this is considered rude. It is customary to fill and refill each other's cups. You pour for your neighbor and he or she will pour for you. It is, therefore, mandatory that you keep checking your friend's cup and ensure it is refilled regularly.

The Japanese people are fine with you not wanting to drink alcohol. Feel free to say no to alcohol and, instead, opt for non-alcoholic beverages such tea, carbonated drinks or juices.

After Eating

After finishing your meal, it is good manners to put everything back on the table the way it was before you started eating. Therefore, it is good etiquette to put the lids back on the dishes, put the chopsticks back on the holder or return them to the paper cover. The term to use after finishing the meal would be *gochisōsama deshita* which translates to '*thank you for the meal or the feast*.' This gratitude is expressed not just to the person who prepared the meal but also to the ingredients of the dishes.

Chapter 5: Public Transport Etiquette

Public transport such as trains and buses are used extensively by the people of Japan and yes, there are rules of etiquette that have to be followed here as well. So, here goes:

Train Etiquette

Getting Off and Getting On

First, allow travelers to get off the train before you board. Ensure you do not stand very close to the door, especially right in front of it while waiting for a train. You are hindering the passageway of the people getting off. Always move inside the car once you have boarded. Don't stand too close to the door because again you will be a hindrance to the people who want to board the train.

When you are getting off the train, ensure you do so in an orderly manner without pushing others. If there are lines to access elevators and escalators, please follow the lines.

During the Travel

The priority seats that are at both the ends of the car (close to the doors) are meant for pregnant women and the elderly. If you are sitting in these seats, you must get up and give your seat when a pregnant woman or an elderly person walks in. In fact, some train lines have ladies-only cars where men are not allowed to board. This approach is to facilitate the prevention of sexual harassment.

You will receive a lot of unhappy frowns if you talk too loudly on the phone or listen to loud music. When you are seated, ensure you occupy only that much place earmarked for one individual. Don't stretch your legs out into the aisle. Sitting on the floor of the train is prohibited as you might hinder the movement of other passengers.

While some trains do allow for travelers to eat and drink, Japanese etiquette is skewed towards avoiding eating and drinking on trains. Even if you have to eat and drink and the particular train line allows it, ensure you don't carry strong-smelling foods and beverages. Also, do not to throw away trash on the train. Keep it wrapped up and put it in a garbage bin at the station you get off.

If children are accompanying you, then you become responsible for their behavior. Ensure you teach your children not to scream and shout and run around on the train. Also, make sure strollers and buggies are kept to the side as much as possible without being too much of a nuisance to the other passengers. When you are traveling with children, it is imperative that you watch out for this: avoid taking more seats than are needed for you and your children. Also, make sure the kids don't stand on the seats with their shoes on.

Bus Etiquette

To ensure that both your and your co-passengers' bus travel is pleasant and safe, bus etiquette in a must-do in Japan. Follow the simple rules given below:

1. Turn down the volume of your headphone or earphones.
2. You should not push the seat in front of you with your legs. It will be very inconvenient to the person sitting in that seat.
3. Your cell phones must either be turned off or kept in silent mode. No one in the bus wants to hear your phone ringing, and no one wants to hear you carry on any conversation on the phone. It is considered unruly and rude to let your phone ring shrilly or talk loudly into it.
4. Even if you are talking to your companion(s) traveling with you on the bus, you must remember to keep your voice down.
5. You should not bring strong-smelling food items. When you sneeze or cough, please do so into a handkerchief, which is covering your nose and mouth.

6. Do not throw trash and garbage away on the bus. Carry it with you and drop it into the first wastebasket you come across after you get off the bus.
7. No fighting is allowed on buses (or trains for that matter).
8. If you are feeling sick, please quickly retrieve the waste bag and use it.
9. If you are planning to recline your seat, make sure you tell the person sitting behind you before push the reclining button.
10. You should not touch or speak to the driver of the bus while he is driving. Wait for the bus to stop to ask questions.
11. No smoking and spitting allowed in the bus.
12. No graffiti or any other form of disfigurement of the bus is allowed.
13. Don't place your luggage or bag in the aisle hindering the smooth movement of other passengers.
14. You are not allowed to put your hand or any other body part outside the bus at any point in time.
15. While seated, please make sure you and your children, if any, are buckled up correctly.
16. Do not walk around in the bus when it is moving.
17. Keep your valuables with you at all times.
18. Seats are ideally assigned in such a way that men and women unknown to each other are not put together. However, there could be instances when you might be separated from your group in the seating arrangement. It would be futile and foolhardy fighting over this point. You must simply sit in your allocated seat and buckle

up without causing a nuisance to anyone else on the bus.

If you can remember that public transport systems are not an individual's private property but have to be shared amicably by all, you will automatically pick up the right etiquette.

Buses in Japan

Chapter 6: Telephone and Email Etiquette

Today, telephones and emails have become part of our culture and the world is your oyster. Each country has its own way of handling telephone and email etiquette. True to its core nature, Japan has quite a stringent etiquette mode for the use of telephone and emails.

Telephone Etiquette in Japan

In Japan, it is common to use the Japanese language to answer phones. It would be inappropriate to speak in a foreign language especially on the phone when the person on the other end does not know your inability to speak the language. This is especially so when you go to work in Japan. One of the first things that your employer will teach is how to answer the phone.

In a formal setting, the 'hello' in Japanese is 'moshi moshi.' It is very commonly used and every phone call has this expression in it. However, in a business context, this is not enough and there are specific words you must use which you will learn while taking your mandatory Japanese language course.

However, here are some basic business telephone etiquette tips for you:

When making a call

You must avoid calling at any of the following times:

- Early in the morning
- When you know it is their lunch time
- In the evening when you know they are going to leave office

If you have called a customer, it is imperative that you first allow the customer to hang up the phone before you put down the phone. Hang up the phone gently and silently.

When answering a phone call

It is customary in Japan to pick up the phone within three rings. If for some reason you took some time to answer the phone, then you must apologize for the delay. When you are passing the call to another colleague, it is important that you put the caller on hold so that he or she doesn't hear the conversation between you and your colleague before transferring the call. Additionally, please ask the caller's permission to put him or her on hold.

It is considered rude to keep the caller waiting for very long. If you know your colleague is not immediately accessible, then offer to take a message or to get your colleague to call back or request the caller to call back. Follow the caller's instructions and do what's needed after finishing the call.

Email Etiquette

Communication through email has become the norm today. Even business contracts and agreements are signed through email. As is normal, the Japanese people have their own etiquette code for using email. Here are a few tips:

Names in your email

Just like how you would address someone as Mr. X in the Western world, you must suffix –san in formal Japanese conversation. So, you will address X as X-san in your email to him. Also, it is important not to combine Mr. and –san because they are essentially one and the same. So, if you combine the two, you will, in effect, be saying Mr. Mr. X, which is weird.

Polite form of communication

Emails in the Japanese business culture are exchanged using the polite form of addressing people and other language aspects. This polite form is called 'keigo.' You must continue to use this form with your Japanese client unless he or she comes back and says that it is not necessary to be so formal. Ideally, this situation will be reached when a certain level of depth in the business relationship is reached.

The keigo form of communication is indicative of the importance of politeness and courtesy expected and delivered by the Japanese people. Even though emails are considered less formal than the written form of communication, starting your email with a polite greeting (which could also be a question on the weather) reflects your understanding of their culture which is bound to make your client happy. The polite greeting is a norm and is expected in all emails.

Stringing

Stringing the original message along with your message is fine. However, if you keep attaching all the older messages in such a way that a whole thread of conversation is created, then it is considered rude and unprofessional in Japan. Your email message will look like *Re:re:re:re:subject* when you string messages.

It is better to start a new message and refer to the earlier messages by writing about them in a couple of sentences so that all parties know what is being spoken about and referred to in this new email. This kind of email response looks professional and neat.

English v Japanese

If you are confident about your Japanese language skills, then it makes a lot of sense to write your emails in that language. Using the Japanese language puts a lot of the Japanese business people at ease. Even though the English language is taught as a mandatory subject in many schools in the country, even the most learned people are not very well-versed in Business English. They also don't speak English on a daily basis. They speak it only during international meetings where others who don't understand Japanese are also present.

However, if you have a problem with Japanese or you prefer English, then you must make a note of this in your email and let your Japanese partner(s) know that all future correspondence will take place in English. You can then write emails in English unless the other party explicitly wants it to be in Japanese.

Age Gap Issues in Communication

The current generation of Japanese is highly tech-savvy and can handle computers and all the latest gadgets. Yet, many of the businesses in Japan are still run by the older generation (or at least they are still in powerful influential positions in the company). These people may not be very computer savvy.

You could choose to send them a note asking to speak either on the phone or in person for a more detailed business meeting. By doing this, you are empowering them to decide while letting them know that you are okay with either option.

Chapter 7: Gift Giving

Replete with ancient folklore and a rich and deep tapestry of culture and history, superstition plays an important role in the life of Japanese people even today, despite the huge strides they have taken in science and technology

Gift-giving is an etiquette that is full of these superstitions and the color, the number, or even the printed animals on your gift wrap can be seen as offensive by many of the Japanese people. It is, therefore, important for you to learn the do's and don'ts of gift-giving etiquette in the country.

Numbers to Avoid during Gift Giving

Do not send gifts with the following numbers associated with them. For example, you cannot send someone four varieties or even four pieces of cake as a gift. Here are the numbers to avoid:

- **Four** – the Japanese word for four sounds like the word for death and, therefore, is taboo to be used in giving gifts.
- **Nine** – sounds like 'suffering' in the Japanese language and should not be involved in gift giving
- **Forty- three** – this number should be completely avoided when gifting for baby showers because the word sounds like 'stillbirth' and can be seen as inauspicious.

A thumb rule is to avoid numbers with 4 or 9 in them.

Animals Considered Auspicious for Gift Giving

The addition of something related to the following animals enhances the meaning of your gift and the receiver will be happy to welcome you.

- **Butterflies** – means longevity and joy
- **Carp** – means faithfulness and good fortune
- **Cranes** – are the perfect animal to incorporate into a wedding gift because they signify good fortune and longevity
- **Swallows** – this bird's tail is considered to bring good luck
- **Turtles** – means longevity and, therefore, great for baby showers

Importance of Colors in Japanese Gift-Giving Etiquette

Colors carry a lot of significance and importance in Japan. You might love writing in black ink but it makes sense to change the color of your ink while writing wishes and compliments on your gift to your Japanese business partner. Here are some insights into colors:

- **Red** - Is used for tombstones. Do not use red ink to sign gift cards. Make sure your Christmas card is not red because red cards are printed for funerals in Japan.
- **Black** - Means death or bad luck. A black and red combination is an expression of sexuality. Avoid it.
- **Green** - Is perfect for all gift-giving occasions because it signifies good luck and eternity
- **White** - Means holy. You can use white ink on another accepted color for baby showers.
- **Purple** - Represents decadence and celebrations. It is a great color to use for festive occasions.

When to Give Gifts

There are multiple occasions in Japan where gift giving is not just a culture, but a form of expected etiquette. Here are some examples of gift-giving occasions:

- Giri choco on Valentine's Day
- Omiyage when you return from a trip
- Gifts are exchanged at the end of the year (oseibo) and mid-year (ochugen) usually to denote gratitude and indebtedness

- You must carry a gift when you are invited to someone's home
- Gifts are also exchanged during other times such as Christmas, weddings, birthdays, etc

How to Give and Receive Gifts

You must carry your gift in a normal shopping bag so that no one will know you are carrying a gift.

When giving or receiving gifts, you must use both your hands.

If the gift is for an individual, then you must find a time when you are alone with the person and give it without the knowledge of others. Moreover, you must give the gift at the end of the visit and not towards the beginning.

While handing over the gift, it is common to say things like 'it's something very small (or boring) but please accept it.' These words denote that the relationship is more important than the gift.

When you give a gift, don't expect the host to open it immediately. He or she will thank you and open it later. Similarly, when you receive gifts, you must not open them immediately. You should open it when you are alone so that you don't have to bother to hide or mask your reaction to the gift, especially if it is something you don't like.

It is polite to reject accepting the gift once or maybe twice. But, if you overdo the non-acceptance part, then it is considered rude.

Make sure your gift is wrapped beautifully. The presentation and your thought behind gifting are more important than the gift itself.

Of course, in an informal setting with close friends and family, these rules do not apply. Gift exchanges in family environments happen in a very casual manner.

Best Kinds of Gifts to Take

Food from your area or region is a great gift to bring to your business partner or client. Food items like cookies and cakes are loved by the Japanese.

For women, flowers are great gifts. But you must remember not to bring white flowers, camellias, lilies and lotus blooms because these are associated with funerals. Avoid potted plants too as they are connected to sickness.

Good quality alcohol or luxury pens or business card holders are great business gifts. However, when you give these gifts, it is important that they don't have your company logo on them.

When you are going to someone's home for a visit, the edibles from your home country are the best form of gift you can take.

Gift-giving is an important form of etiquette in Japan, which has to be followed diligently and as per accepted norms.

Chapter 8: Temple or Shrine Visiting Etiquette

Visiting shrines, temples, and other places of worship is an important Japanese tradition. During important occasions, especially New Year's Day, you will see long lines of people waiting to enter a holy shrine to pray for a good year. Here are some tips on how to behave correctly in a temple or shrine. Visiting and praying at shrines is called omairi and if this is done specifically for New Year, the ritual is called hatsu-moude.

Differences between a Shrine and a Temple

In Japan, there are clear differences between the two structures even though they appear to be the same. Here are some important differences:

- Shrines (Jinja) have a simple gate structure called the 'torii' whereas the gates of a temple (Tera) referred to as sanmon lead to a separate house by itself.
- There are Buddhist statues and images in temples whereas shrines do not have these images.
- Shrines are sacred Shinto sites whereas temples are sacred Buddhist sites.

Etiquette for Visiting a Shrine

As you approach the torii of the shrine, take care to walk on the side and not in the middle of the path as it is believed that the middle path and the torii are reserved for the gods.

Near the entrance of a shrine, you will see a chozuya, a little pavilion with a basin of water, where you should purify yourself before going to the main shrine. First, fill a ladle (many are kept near the basin) with water and pour a little into your left hand and cleanse it. Then, pour out a little water from the same ladle into your right hand and cleanse it. Then, you must cleanse your mouth also ensuring you do not take water directly from the ladle.

Instead, pour out some water into your left hand and use that to clean your mouth. When this is done, hold the ladle in an upright position so that the remaining water will trickle down the handle and clean it too. Then put the ladle back. Even in winter, this cleansing ritual has to be done before walking into the main shrine.

The following steps can be followed when you are in front of the main shrine:

- First, bow slightly. Put a coin into the coin box in front. Remember to be gentle when you drop the coin. The amount of money you put in doesn't matter. Even a 5-yen is sufficient to accompany your wishes and prayers to the deity of the shrine.
- Ring the bell twice or thrice. This is a symbol of letting the deity know you have arrived.
- At this stage, do a 90-degree deep bow. Now clap your hands twice with your right hand slightly at the back.
- Say your prayers for your wishes and remember to include gratitude too. Deeply bow one last time.

Etiquette for Visiting a Temple

The process of entering (by the side and not the middle) and the cleansing at the chozuya is the same as when visiting a shrine. The differences are in the way you worship here. Here are a few etiquette tips to follow while worshipping at a Japanese temple:

- Burning incense is an expected part of worship in Japanese temples, as it is believed that the smell of incense is actually food for the Buddha. You must not light your incense from the burning end of someone else's stick. This is equivalent to taking on the sins of the other person.
- Bow slight and gently drop a coin in the coin box. If there is a bell, ring it twice or thrice for the same reason as done in a shrine.

- Pay your respects to the Buddha and join your palms in front of your chest as a symbol of respect and reverence. You must NOT clap in temples.
- You will see many devotees holding a string of beads while praying. You can do it too. Remember to include gratitude in your prayers

After finishing your prayers and paying respects at the shrine and temple, you can do the following if you wish:

- You can buy an *ema, which* is a wooden plank on which you can write your prayers and wishes and hang it up at the designated place so that it can be received by the gods.
- You can buy *hamaya* or the holy arrows to be hung at home. These arrows are believed to ward off evil spirits.
- Amulets or *omamori* can also be bought which are believed to have powers to facilitate safe driving and easy delivery.
- Shuin are commemorative stamps that can be offered at shrines and temples as a symbol of your visit there.
- *Omikuji* is a small piece of paper with your fortune written on it. You can buy this and either keep it at home or hang it in the temple or shrine. Most of these fortune-telling papers are in Japanese but some temples and shrines have English versions too. *Omikuji* fortunes are varied and some of them include:
  - ➢ Dai-kichi or great blessing
  - ➢ Sho-kichi or small blessing
  - ➢ Chuu-kichi or middle blessing
  - ➢ Kichi or blessing
  - ➢ Sue-kichi or ending blessing

- ➢ Kyo or curse
- ➢ Dai-kyo or big curse

Omikuji fortunes also give advice, remedies, and suggestions for various aspects of your life including relationships, travel, wishes and health. So, the next time you visit a Japanese shrine or temple, focus less on taking pictures and more on the wonderful, spiritual experience of the place by following the steps mentioned in this chapter.

Chapter 9: Tea Culture Etiquette

A Japanese tea ceremony goes beyond the tea that is consumed. Every aspect of the ceremony including the seating arrangement, the cleaning of the utensils and tools, the scooping up of the tea leaves at the end and every other element in between holds a lot of significance. It reflects the importance of appreciating every step and everyone involved in the process starting from the host, the guests, and the other elements of the tea ceremony. Let us look at the etiquette tips for the highly revered ceremony in Japan.

The Tea Room

The Japanese tea ceremony is referred to as Sado, Chanoyu, or Ocha. The ceremony is actually a choreographic ritual involving the preparation and serving of Matcha, or Japanese green tea. To balance the bitter taste of green tea, Japanese sweets are served as accompaniments during the ceremony.

There are pre-defined movements and gestures to be strictly adhered to while pouring out the tea. The process is more than the act of drinking tea. It deals with the aesthetics of the entire process and the appreciation involved. It reflects the Japanese culture of doing everything from the core of their hearts including the seemingly mundane task of preparing and serving tea.

Everything in the tearoom is placed from the guests' viewpoint. The angles of the utensils, the placement, etc. are all done with the intention of the guests getting maximum benefit. There is almost always a main guest in the tea ceremony referred to as *Shokyaku*.

Tea ceremonies differ in their process, format, and the tea and accompaniments served depending on the season. The tea ceremony during winter season involves preparing the tea in a sunken square hole called Ro made on the Tatami floor. The Kama or the iron kettle is placed in the Ro during the winter. During summer, the Kama is put on a brazier.

Moreover, charcoal procedure (called Sumi-demae) is also different in summer and winter. The utensils are placed differently and at different locations in summer and winter. Therefore, the process of finishing the tea ceremony also differs between the two seasons.

The actual process of making tea is very basic and simple. Yet, every gesture and every moment is predefined and calls for strict adherence. The tea ceremony is steeped in spirituality and in a silent and serene atmosphere.

The Most Basic Elements of Etiquette

- Always be on time. Do **NOT** arrive late for the tea ceremony.
- You will have to remove your shoes outside. Your host will invariably provide you with slippers specifically kept for use in tea ceremonies
- While the Japanese kimono is the preferred dress to be worn for tea ceremonies, it is also allright if you come in conservative and formal western wear. However, if you can manage a kimono, your host will be thrilled.

Etiquette Tips While in the Tea Room

When you are inside the tearoom, there are specific rules of etiquette to follow. They are:

- Do not sit in any place of your choosing. Wait until the host seats you at your designated place.
- You must enter on your knees and not walking on your feet. Avoid stepping on the middle of the mats. Use fists

and not open palms while touching the mats. This is for hygiene purposes.

- When the teacup comes to you, remember to turn the cup slightly to avoid putting your lips at the same place the previous person had drunk from. Again, this is for hygiene.
- Eat everything that is offered to you.

The Act of Appreciation

The seating arrangement, decided by the host, in a tearoom holds a lot of significance. The main guest, the *Shokyaku*, is the person who is in charge of communicating with the host. He is the person responsible for showing appreciation for the efforts of the host. Even if you are not the primary guest, you must focus on appreciating things that you see around you.

Look around the tearoom and the notice all the elements kept there. Each of those elements is significant in its own right. Make an effort to be curious and ask pertinent questions. You can ask questions and show appreciation about the teacups, the flowers and the scrolls, or anything else of interest and pass on the message to the host through the *Shokyaku*. It is important not to be frivolous and simply say something nice for the sake of it. Make an effort to be honest and sincerely curious about the tea ceremony and its various elements.

Silence and serenity are two of the most important things to maintain in a tea ceremony. There are many other less formal drinking occasions you will find in Japan. Leave raucous partying to those places and occasions. Within the sacred precinct of a tearoom, it is imperative that you maintain silence and present a serene and dignified presence.

Focus on the appreciation aspect of the tea ceremony. Pay attention to the various elements of the room and the process and open your heart and mind while participating in the tea ceremony. It is an honor to be invited to one such ceremony and it is up to you to take full advantage of the beauty and elegance right from the beginning until the time you leave the tearoom.

Chapter 10: Apologizing in Japanese Culture

Saying sorry is a social etiquette that is expected to be followed in almost every culture of the world. And yet, the concept of apology in Japan is not merely a form of etiquette but is a non-negotiable social expectation. The concept of saying sorry first in Japan is not based on the person's sense of sorrow or regret but is meant to facilitate smoothing over of any conflicts in the social setup.

Even if you did not do anything wrong or did not make a mistake, saying sorry is a way to maintain harmony. It avoids unnecessary feelings of embarrassment and awkwardness at home, at your workplace, or among friends and family.

In the corporate world of Japan, this concept of apology is taken to an altogether new level. Here is an example of how seriously apologies are taken in Japanese organizations. For example, if an employee dies at the workplace because of negligence from the company's side, the CEO is expected to visit the bereaved family and offer condolences and apologies. This entire exercise is broadcast on TV and through other media as well.

Different Types of Apology in the Japanese Culture

There are many types of apologies in the Japanese culture and here are a few of them:

Gomenasai

The Japanese expression to formally say sorry is 'Gomenasai.' It is a word that reflects sincere and heartfelt apology. However, the use of this expression is restricted to very close family and friends. It is not a common thing for the Japanese people to apologize using 'Gomenasai' to strangers and or even to seniors. It is used by colleagues, family members, and close friends.

Moushiwake gozaimasen deshita

Another expression used for a formal apology is 'Moushiwake gozaimasen deshita' which is reserved only for really grave mistakes. Used in businesses and corporations, this expression is commonly used between business houses and their clients. It is also used commonly in situations resulting serious consequences and repercussions for people. A classic example where '*Moushiwake gozaimasen deshita*' is used is if production was delayed for a client resulting in losses or something similar.

Sumimasen

This is most commonly used expression for saying sorry in daily life. You can use it when you have inadvertently stepped on someone's toes. You can also use this expression in place of 'excuse me' in situations such as calling a waiter or asking for space to move in or out of a crowded train. This expression says 'Sorry for the inconvenience and thank you for your support.'

A word of caution when you use this expression: there is a slang version '*suimasen*' or the even shortened version '*suman.*' This slang version should not be used when talking to seniors and superiors as it reflects a casualness that is frowned upon in all formal settings.

Sumimasen deshita

This expression takes the level of apology to a deeper level than 'sumimasen.' This expression of apology is used when bigger mistakes than inconveniences are committed. It is used to say sorry to superiors for an error made by you. The 'deshita' makes it past tense and loosely translates to 'I am sorry for what I did.'

Gomen, Gomen Nasai, and Gomen kudasai

The meaning of 'men' in Gomen is 'to forgive.' Therefore, these three words are expressions of apology in ascending order of keigo. This expression reflects a sense of accepting the wrongdoing by requesting forgiveness. Gomen nasai and gomen kudasai are more polite terms (please forgive me) of apology as compared to plain gomen.

Sumimasen and gomen nasai can be treated as equivalent forms of saying sorry. However, as the latter term includes an expression of acceptance of guilt, it is more appropriate to use for superiors and elders than the former.

Shitsurei and Shitsurei-shimasu

Translating to 'pardon my rudeness' this expression is used while excusing yourself from a person of respect and dignity. For example, if you are leaving your doctor's clinic after consulting with him or her, you would use this expression.

Makotoni-moushiwake-gozaimasen-deshita

This is, perhaps, a very strong form of apology and translates to 'I am totally responsible for my mistakes and there are no excuses for it and I sincerely regret my mistake.' This expression is used to apologize to the public through public announcements usually for train and bus delays. But it is not used commonly in the day-to-day life.

The Dogeza

The gesture of dogeza is a way of showing very deep respect to the other person. It is a deeply grounded aspect of Japanese etiquette. Although the word means 'sitting on the ground,' for the Japanese it is a custom that goes beyond sitting on the floor. In the modern Japanese world, it is used very rarely and the younger Japanese generation does not use it all as such intense situations of apology rarely arise in today's world.

The dogeza bow involves kneeling on the floor and bringing your head down to touch the floor while holding your open palms on the ground. It is an expression of sincere and deep apology and was used by people in the lower strata of society to people in the higher strata of society.

For example, a person who has committed a crime performs dogeza not to simply ask for forgiveness but to plead and beg for it. In the earlier times, a peasant would perform dogeza in front of his landlord to show the deep need for the loan that he is asking for. While this gesture does seem to have a demeaning connotation, the positive side is that the person receiving the dogeza is inclined to forgive and forget after getting such a sincere and deep form of apology.

Chapter 11:
Visiting a Japanese Home

Every home is a sanctuary offering privacy, joy, and succor to the family members. When you are invited to someone's home, it is a matter of honor that the person and his or her family consider you for the invitation into their sanctuary. We all have rules and regulations within our homes and expect our guests to follow them to their best ability.

Similarly, in Japan too, there are rules of etiquette to be followed when visiting a home. As an esteemed visitor, when you make the effort to follow etiquette, not only is your behavior reflecting the strength of your character and your culture, you are telling your host that you value and respect his or her traditions. This chapter is dedicated to giving you some general rules of etiquette to be followed when visiting a Japanese home.

Don't Be Late

The Japanese culture frowns upon lack of discipline and punctuality is taken very seriously. While the cultures of other countries believe in being on time for all events, in Japan, punctuality is a little stricter. You being late for the home visit will affect their other schedules for the day. Of course, a few minutes after the appointed time is fine especially considering the delays caused by traffic.

If, however, you are going to be late by more than a quarter of an hour, you must call ahead, explain the reason for your delay, and apologize for the inconvenience. While being on time is important, you must remember not to arrive too early as it would be an inconvenience to the family members who will be engaged in cooking, cleaning, and tidying up for your visit.

Don't Bring Along Uninvited Guests without Permission

Suppose you are invited to a party or gathering to someone's home and you want to take a friend or your spouse along with you. You are expected to get permission from your host in advance before you take along other guests. Coming for the visit with extra people without getting permission is not allowed and is considered being disrespectful.

While your hosts may not openly refuse or object to the presence of uninvited guests, it goes without saying that they are going to be highly inconvenienced as they will not have made arrangements for the extra people who came unannounced. You already know how strict the Japanese culture is about seating arrangements, dinner etiquette, etc. Last minute changes to these arrangements can be quite a challenge.

Always Carry a Gift

Refer to the chapter on gift-giving etiquette and recall the importance of carrying a gift for your hosts when you visit them. Fruit or snacks from your home country will be highly appreciated. It doesn't have to be something big or expensive. It can be small and sweet. Just remember to gift-wrap and present it well.

Announce Your Arrival

You already know that saying hello when you enter someone's house is customary in many homes across different cultures. Japan is similar, too, and the common greeting you give when you arrive is *Ojama shimasu*, which translates to 'sorry for disturbing you.' This greeting reflects your humility and gratitude to your host for having you in his or her home.

Remove Your Shoes

One of the most important elements of a Japanese home is the 'no shoes inside the home' policy. There is usually a designated space near the entrance of the house where you must keep your shoes before entering the home. There are home slippers that your host will give you, which you can wear, inside the house. However, some homes might not have extra slippers for guests. It would be a good idea to carry a pair in your bag.

Also, it is important that you wear stockings or socks. Not wearing socks or stockings is considered rude. Most Japanese homes have separate slippers for using the restroom. Slip them on when you use the restroom and switch back to your home slippers when you are out of the toilet.

If you are entering a room with tatami mats, then the home slippers also have to be removed outside the room. When leaving your host's home after the event, remember to put the home slippers back in the same place and in the same manner you found them.

Don't Sit without Permission

Seating arrangements in Japanese homes are very strict. Everyone in the home and from the guest list would have been allocated specific seats. So, if you sit without permission, you could be running the risk of usurping someone else's seat. It is prudent to ask for permission before sitting or stand until you are guided by your host to your allocated seat.

Table Manners

Look up the chapter on Dining Etiquette for more information on this. However, you can also observe and watch how others are behaving at the table and follow suit. The Japanese people love to pass on their compliments to the chef by expressing how delicious the food is. The expression for this is 'umai' or 'oishii'.

Your silence, despite the fact that you are enjoying the food, is not allowed. You must express your love for the food and keep on passing compliments to the chef. However, if you don't like a particular type of food, you don't need to pretend. You can say politely that you are not very fond of that kind of food and excuse yourself. This attitude is perfectly allowed and your host will appreciate your honesty. Just remember not to react negatively to any dish or food item.

Offer to Help in the Clearing-Up Activity

After the meal is over, don't simply say goodbye and walk out. You must offer to stay back and offer to clear up the table and help with the cleaning of the dishes too. Even if the host insists that it is not needed, you must make the offer because it is polite to do so. It is quite likely that your host will simply ask you to relax and enjoy the post-meal conversation with the other guests and the members of the family. If so, remember to mingle with everyone and try to make small talk thereby appreciating their gesture of inviting you into their private sanctuary.

Don't Stay Beyond a Decent Time

Making yourself overly comfortable after a great Japanese meal sounds like a great idea to you but it will most likely be considered impolite by your host. Do not overstay your welcome. Putting up your feet, taking a nap and giving the impression that you do not respect your host's time and space is considered rude behavior. So, leave when you know that everything about the visit is over and done with.

Chapter 12: Relationship and Dating Etiquette in Japan

The dating and relationship culture in Japan is quite unique. Although the dating scene is casual and fun, there are some strict forms of etiquette that have to be followed in order for you to be accepted in the Japanese society.

Don't Make a Spectacle of Your Date or Relationship

Blending in with the environment and modesty are two important elements of Japanese relationships. It is considered rude and embarrassing if you make a spectacle of your relationship and dating events. If you are interested in taking up a relationship with a man or woman, then you must do so in private and discreetly. Find out the person's phone number and call them up. Showing your affection in public is frowned upon.

First Dates Decorum

The standard dinner followed by a movie is the perfect first date which can hardly go wrong in Japan. However, even simple and cheap dates focusing on togetherness and fun, such as a picnic in the park, are considered a romantic thing to do in Japanese society. Glamour and extravagance are not necessary elements to a good first date.

A round of karaoke is always a great idea. Your ability and courage to take center stage and sing even if your voice is not that great is considered a humble trait and humility is a highly respected personality characteristic in Japan.

Gender Roles in Japan Are Quite Different From the Rest of the World

Unlike the rest of the world where the men take center-stage in terms of taking action, in Japan, the women are open, vulnerable and active about letting their feelings be known. Men, on the other hand, are expected to show restraint and reflect calm and poise in their behavior. Men are not really allowed to express their feelings very openly. This is the reason why women are the first ones to confess love and also pay for their dates instead of the way it is done in the West.

In fact, men are simply supposed to sit and wait patiently while the women run around and find ways and means of confessing their love. Japanese women don't hesitate to do everything in their power to get close to a man they desire.

While feeling hurt if rejected by the man is common, it hardly creates a dent in the confidence and power of Japanese women as they will try harder for the next available man! Women in Japan chase men they desire through acts of kindness and through gift-giving and doing everything else for the man they love.

Friends' Approval is Important

As weird as it might seem for the non-Japanese person, in Japan, friends are as important as the dating relationships you keep. Friends play a very important role in the society of Japan. They are the ones who shape and mold your personality. Before taking your chosen partner on a private date, you must first take him or her to go to group parties and get-togethers and get the approval of your friends. It is indeed a unique cultural aspect of dating in Japan.

Physical Intimacy Takes Time

Unlike the Western culture where physical intimacy is considered a form of showing your affection, in Japanese societies, hugging, kissing or even touching cannot take place until the partners get the boyfriend/girlfriend status. Until then, no physical intimacy is allowed.

Age of the Your Date Matters

People who were born and brought up during the '80s and early '90s made a lot of money and their expectations with regard to gifts can be quite expensive. Lack of expensive gifts could be seen as an absence of love. However, the younger generation who are brought up in a more frugal environment have learned to scale down their expectations quite a bit.

Who Pays the Bill?

Although in the standard Japanese dining etiquette, everyone shares equally, on a date, usually the man pays. However, remember that the women in Japan are more vocal than the men and so if she insists on making the payment or dividing the bill equally more than twice, then it is for the men to stop arguing and do as bidden.

Basic Table Manners are Expected While Dining

Remember to say *itadakimasu* before the meal and *gotchisosama deshita* after the meal. Refer to dining etiquette for more information. It is imperative that you follow proper table manners and etiquette to impress your Japanese date.

Foreign Men Are Liked Whereas Foreign Women Are Still Not Popular

The women in Japan find foreign men exotic and lovable and many women actually love the idea of a half-western and half-Japanese child. Therefore, foreign men will not have too much of a problem finding a female partner in Japan.

On the contrary, foreign women might find it difficult to get a male partner. There are high expectations from foreign women including that they should speak fluent Japanese and they should scale down their independence a bit. Japanese men are usually known to be a bit rigid on these two stances. However, there are no hard and fast rules. Make the effort and leave the rest to nature, Gods, and the Buddha.

After marriage, it is a strict form of family etiquette for the man to provide for his family while the woman will be responsible for household chores. Though, with modernization taking place at a really fast rate, there could be some changes to this outlook.

Chapter 13:
Business Etiquette

The business etiquette in Japan is often a misunderstood concept by the rest of the world. There are misconceptions that even the most basic business meeting has to have the same level of formality as a tea ceremony. This is far from the truth. The business etiquette in Japan is almost the same as in other countries and includes elements such as sensitivity and good behavior and manners.

However, since the approach to business meetings is more formal than in other countries, it is more obvious. For a Westerner, the first business meeting in Japan could come across as a bit of a culture shock because of the importance of the hierarchical structure in Japanese business houses. Even the seemingly simple act of exchanging business cards has a ritualistic attitude here. Yet, the core of the ritual is based on courtesy, politeness, and sensitivity to the feelings of the other party.

Japanese Business Cards

Business cards in Japan are a must-have element. It must be double-sided with one side in Japanese and the other side in English. Ensure the design on both sides of the card is the same. Even if your business card is not in English and is, perhaps, in German or Italian or French, it is recommended that for doing business effectively in Japan, you print English-Japanese business cards specifically for the country.

The following list can be a good guideline for how many cards to carry for your Japanese business trip:

- At a small meeting, you might be handing out 3-4 cards
- At a large meeting, you might be handing out 10-12 cards
- At a trade show, you might be handing out over 100 cards
- At a conference, you might be handing out over 50 cards

Important Tips to Remember Regarding Business Cards

- Pushing, flicking, or throwing your business card across the table is simply NOT allowed in Japanese business etiquette because it reflects a callous attitude and suggests that you have no pride for the company you represent.
- Present the business card with both your hands reverently with the Japanese side facing upward. Having your company logo at the top corner will enhance the look and presentation of the card.
- In the same way, use both your hands to accept a business card offered to you by your Japanese partner and/or client and say, 'thank you.' At the first meeting, it might make sense to speak in English unless you are fluent in Japanese. If you are not fluent in Japanese, speaking it at the first meeting might break the ice. However, it also runs the risk of confusing the Japanese party. Avoiding it is better.

- At the first meeting, the Japanese side of the business will introduce their team in descending order of importance. It is better to wait for the introductions to take place before handing out business cards as otherwise you might end up mistakenly giving it to a junior before the senior which can be considered as a slight on your part.
- Don't use the Japanese business cards to make notes. Make your notes elsewhere. Also, don't fidget, play with, or bend the business cards given to you. Put them in a card case and treat them with respect.
- At the end of the meeting, remember to pick up all the business cards from the table. Leaving cards behind is a huge insult and it implies that you don't consider the person important enough to take the card along with you.
- Don't get carried away with the position of the person and make the mistake of leaving behind cards of juniors in the company. Remember that in Japan, an employee will stay with the same company for a very long time because that is the work culture there. In about 10-15 years, that person you slighted could be responsible for a huge budget and he or she will remember that slight which could turn out nasty for you.

Business Attire in Japan

- Business attire is more or less fixed for men in Japan.
- From October until April, the business attire consists of black, dark navy, or charcoal gray suits in combination with white shirts and a subdued tie.

- Do not wear the combination of black suit, black tie, and white shirt as this attire is for funerals only
- In the winter months (from December until February), formal coats are used as part of the business attire. During the rainy season (March and April), short raincoats are used.
- During the months of May until September, the dark suits are replaced with light gray suits.
- Short well-groomed hairstyles are sported for a business look. Excessive use of cologne or aftershave is considered taboo. Most of the companies in Japan do not allow their men to grow a beard or shave their heads. While there are no strict rules for women's attire as it is only recently that women in Japan moved into corporate life, the following tips will help:
- Avoid excessive glamor including bright-colored handbags or carry bags.
- Wear your hair short or tie it back if it is very long
- Long skirt suits or trouser suits in the same color combination as mentioned above will work well
- Avoid short skirts, high heels, and jewelry too

Business Meetings Etiquette

Face-to-face business meetings are very important in Japanese culture. Here are some etiquette tips on conducting meetings with your Japanese clients and partners:

- Plan a detailed and precise agenda for the meeting. If the meeting agenda says that it will be finished at 3 p.m., then ensure it finishes at that time. Japanese businessmen generally have very tight daily schedules

- English language presentations should not be used. Presentations have to be translated into the Japanese language
- Make sure all the important points are detailed clearly in your presentation slides. The Japanese businessmen believe that all important elements of the business are in the slide and if an element is not in the slide, then it is not important
- Take printouts of your presentation to be handed out to the people attending the meeting
- Always use the services of a Japanese interpreter. Not only are you respecting the Japanese culture and their language but also letting them know that it is important to you that they fully comprehend what is happening in the meeting
- Late arrivals are not allowed. But, if for some compelling reason you are going to be delayed, it is imperative you call about 45 minutes to one hour before the appointed time
- Seating arrangements are pre-arranged, so don't take a seat until you are guided to your seat

Chapter 14:
Feedback and Criticism Etiquette

It might come across as strange to many non-Japanese, but, it is true that positive feedback is not really appreciated in Japanese culture. In fact, if you were to speak to non-Japanese who have worked with Japanese bosses and/or subordinates, their initial reaction to this unique trait of the Japanese people would have been 'shock.'

The logic behind this is simple. If the Japanese have to give praise, it has to be 100% perfect and considering the fact that nothing in this world can be so and also that no matter how well you do a job, there is always room for improvement, praise is not easily given by Japanese bosses. On the contrary, if you have Japanese subordinates, praise from you can be taken as appearing ingratiating, which is not also appreciated in Japanese culture. Therefore, positive feedback is neither given nor received in the Japanese corporate world.

Positive feedback is frowned upon by the Japanese because of their *homegoroshi* belief. The root of 'home' in this Japanese expression is 'homeru' or praise and the root of 'goroshi' is korosu or kill. Therefore, homegoroshi means praise-kill! It is nothing but a backhanded compliment. In Japan, there is a special ironical tone used to say praise in such a way that it is actually meant to damage.

The praise appears so only on the surface but beneath the basic meaning, so it is actually an attack, which is not easy to fight back. This kind of underhand praise has come to be taken very seriously and even genuinely meant positive feedback is taken in this manner. Therefore, as a rule, it is better not to give praise or positive feedback to your Japanese subordinate.

In fact, they go one step further. If you are a boss to a subordinate and he or she gives you an update on the work allocated, it is best to simply read it, ensure you are satisfied and simply say 'thank you.' Now, suppose you are reporting to a Japanese boss. If he or she is asking you for an update on any project or job, then you must take it that your boss is giving you negative feedback. Giving updates is your job and if you have failed, this request is a stern reminder to you of your responsibilities.

Additionally, if your boss comes to ask you how you are doing, how work is progressing, or if everything alright, then it means there is something wrong. Japanese bosses are not known to compliment or praise their team members or subordinates primarily because they believe there is no need to. Moreover, the term 'feedback' did not even exist in Japanese vocabulary before the Western culture brought its influence into the country.

They had to create a new term for feedback during the Meiji era when Westerners first interacted with the Japanese. They gave the term 'fidobakku' for feedback when they were communicating with the Westerners. However, even today, they do not give positive feedback to their Japanese subordinates who, in turn, treat positive feedback warily.

Feedback, positive or otherwise, is part of the Western culture and goes against the collective outlook of Japanese society. It is believed that feedback tends to pit team members against each other, and it is more important to think of the entire organization or group instead of one individual. The Japanese corporate mentality runs like this: "If my company does well, so will I."

Yet, it is very, very important for all team members to keep their superiors informed about the progress of their given task/job. Every matter, irrespective of how trivial it may seem, must be reported to the superiors. This attitude of reporting every trivial matter to the superiors is called *hou-ren-sou* and reflects a deep respect for the system in the organization.

So, how do people give positive feedback? Well, the best thing that employees get in the form of positive feedback is to go out with the boss for a drink as a team. One-to-one sit-downs are not common at all. In fact, if someone is called to be spoken in private, then it means that something is wrong and the employee is bound to panic.

Instead of such a complex way of handling feedback, simply take your team out for a drink. This tradition of bosses and subordinates going for a drink together is called *nomikai*. This kind of party goes on into the late hours toward midnight. Even discussions at such places will focus only on what went wrong so that corrective measures can be taken to prevent the recurrence of the error in the future.

Singling people out to give praise is also not allowed in Japanese corporate culture. Many non-Japanese bosses have burned their fingers by making the mistake of singling out people who have done a good job. Even if the praise was deserved, the person singled out will not feel good about it because he or she will not be trusted by the co-workers or team members anymore!

Singling out one person from a team for praise is considered wrong and it is believed unnecessary competition among the team members will arise resulting in loss of productive and actual work being done. So, it is a done thing that in Japanese culture, positive feedback is avoided and mistakes are discussed in such a way that people can learn from them and corrective measures can be taken.

Chapter 15: Funeral Customs

Funerals are, of course, difficult times for everyone, especially the bereaved family. There are clear-cut etiquette rules to be followed while being part of an Ososhiki, as a Japanese funeral is called. Irrespective of which religion the Japanese family belongs to, the funeral ceremony is conducted in the Buddhist style. Almost all forms of funerals are cremation-based and in fact, some local governments even ban burials in the community.

It is essential to remember that you have to be invited to a funeral. You can neither invite yourself nor can you go uninvited. Here are a few etiquette tips to be followed while attending a Japanese funeral.

There are basically two ceremonies including the Wake (or the Otsuya) and the funeral ceremony (or the Ososhiki). In the Otsuya, the members of the bereaved family and the invited friends and relatives spend time with the body of the deceased person paying their respects. It is allright for many people who cannot attend the actual funeral to come only for the otsuya to pay their respects and leave before the Ososhiki starts.

The Ososhiki usually starts after the day of Otsuya and consists of many ceremonies. There are priests who chant sutras and incense sticks are burned by the members of the family. The final cremation ceremony is usually very private and only the closest family members are allowed here. The family members pick out the bones (using chopsticks) from the ashes after the cremation. They place these bones in an urn, which is then interned in the family grave.

What to Wear to the Funeral

Like in most countries, black is the mourning color in Japan too. It is very important to come suitably attired for a Japanese funeral. Not being correctly attired is seen as a sign of disrespect.

Attire for Men

Plain black suits tailored in conservative style, black tiees, and white shirts are the ultimate funeral attire. Black shoes that are not shiny or ornamental in any way should be worn. No jewelry except wedding rings is allowed at a funeral.

Attire for Women

Black kimono or any kind of black conservative attire is allowed for women. There should be no patterns on the dress, and no lace or frills either. There should be anything shiny or ornamental in the dress. The hem should fall below the knee, should have a high neck, and should not be form-fitting.

You should wear fully closed plain black shoes with no shiny buckles or any other form of ornamentation. Black nylon stockings that are opaque; no see-throughs allowed. Except for your wedding ring and, perhaps, a plain single pearl string, no jewelry is allowed for women either. Makeup should be avoided or very understated with no evidence of loud lipstick or heavy perfume. If you have long hair, please fold it into a bun and short hair should be kept down using hairspray. Bags, if any, should also be plain black.

What to Bring to the Funeral

Condolence money, or okoden, is given to the bereaved family by the attending guests as funeral offerings. The amount varies between 3000 Yen and 30000 Yen depending on many factors including your relationship with the deceased and his or her family, the financial and social status of the bereaved family and the mourner.

You are free to use your judgment with regard to the amount of okoden. You must only remember that you should NOT put crisp new notes into the collection because it will then be believed that you expected the death to take place and, therefore, had the time to get new notes ready for the occasion! Do NOT give new notes.

Also, it is extremely important to put the money in an opaque envelope. You simply cannot give the money openly for all to see. It would be better not to give at all rather than give without a discreet envelope.

If you are not able to make it to the funeral, please call ahead and inform the bereaved family along with the reason as to why you cannot come. At this time, you can ask if you can send something in lieu of your presence and if they want something, they will say so. Avoid sending condolence flowers as it is not considered appropriate in Japanese culture.

What to Do During the Ceremony

When you arrive for the funeral ceremony, you will be received by the member(s) of the bereaved family. At this point in time, you must ensure your okoden envelope is out of sight. It is inappropriate to hand over the condolence immediately on arrival. Pay your respects to everyone and wait silently without excessive talking. You can use any of the following condolences messages:

- Goshuushou-sama desu – Your grief at this point must be terrible
- O-kuyami moushiagemas – I offer my condolences.

After greeting the family and paying your respects, you will be guided to the registry to make an entry of your name. There will be a tray placed near the registry for the okoden. You can put your envelope in this tray. After you have entered your name in the registry, you will be shown to your seat. Do not sit where you please as seating arrangements (as in all Japanese events and ceremonies) are predetermined. After the funeral ceremony, you can light the incense by following how others are doing it.

After the Funeral Ceremony

After the ceremony is over, on your way out, you will be offered a token gift in return for your okoden. Only close family members will attend the actual cremation. It is important to remember that you must not go straight to your house or someone else's house directly after a funeral. You must first visit a public place like a park or a family restaurant and then make your way home. This is rooted in the belief the spirit of the dead tends to follow you and you must lead it astray. Otherwise, it will follow you to your home!

Chapter 16: Wedding Etiquette

You will be invited to attend a wedding only if you have become really close to the Japanese family. There are basically two types of weddings that take place in Japan; the traditional Shinto style and the White Wedding Style (which follows at least in appearance a Christian wedding). Irrespective of which style the wedding is going to take place, the etiquette rules are the same.

RSVP

Before you even begin preparing for the wedding, the first thing you must do is send your RSVP. Nearly all Japanese wedding cards come with a reply slip that you must send back to the person who has invited you. It is very important that you complete this card with appropriate words (you cannot go wrong with 'congratulations') and send it back without fail. It might make sense to take extra care and avoid words that imply 'cutting' or 'breaking' in your RSVP message.

The Wedding Gift

In Japan, a wedding gift is nothing but cash delivered in the right way. Even if you cannot attend the wedding, Japanese etiquette calls for you to send the wedding gift correctly wrapped. There are no wedding gift lists to follow as in the case of the Western culture. Cash is the only gift that is considered appropriate for a Japanese wedding.

The minimum amount expected to be given is 30000 Yen though you can reduce the amount if you cannot attend the wedding for any reason. Bosses who attend the weddings of their subordinates are expected to shell out 50000 Yen.

The cash for the wedding gift should be put into a standard wedding envelope, which is called a *shugibukuro*. These are available at all department and stationery stores. Just remember to pick the right envelope in case you pick one meant for funerals. Unlike the funeral okoden, wedding gifts should be given in the form of crisp new notes. You must put your name on the cover and hand it over to the allocated wedding receptionist.

What to Wear

While a formal kimono is a good idea to wear for a wedding, it is important that you know how to wear it perfectly before you try it. Other than that, the only restriction is on the color white.

You should not wear white for a wedding. Black and all other colors are acceptable. Women are generally expected to wear flats or subdued heels and ensure their shoulders, knees, and toes are not revealed. For men, black or any other sensible color suit with a matching tie works well.

Who Can Accompany You to the Wedding?

If the wedding invitation card says you can bring your partner along to the function, remember you must bring only your 'officially recognized' partner. She or he must be known in the social circles as your partner. Your partner should match your gift amount. However, it must be noted that wedding invites are for single entry only because only you will be known to the bride or groom. Moreover, weddings are expensive affairs and, therefore, keeping guest lists small is a commonly done thing in Japanese culture. It is common to see people coming for weddings alone without their partner in Japan.

Wedding Banquet and Reception

As is expected, Japanese weddings will take place at strictly scheduled times with the events clearly specified (along with the duration) in a separate printout. This will be handed over to you once you have registered your attendance. The wedding banquet follows a pattern that is similar to Western weddings and includes speeches from the couple and friends, ring exchanges, cake cutting, etc.

After you finish your meal, remember to take that little bag kept under your chair. This is a gift from the newly-wedded couple as a form of gratitude for your presence. This gift is usually a sweet or a pastry and is referred to as *hikigashi*. Of course, fancier weddings could have fancier gifts. When you finish and pick up your gift, the newly-wedded couple and their parents will be waiting to see you off at the exit even as they thank you for coming. You must return the thanks and pay compliments to the wonderful ceremony.

Another common feature of Japanese weddings is the after-party or the *nijikai*. Only a very small and close group of friends will be invited to this after-party. If you are invited, be ready to shell out another wedding gift amounting to at least 10000 Yen. There will be food and drink at this rather casual party, and it makes sense not to get overly drunk and create a nuisance.

Thank You

When all the festivities are over and done with, you must remember to send a follow-up thank you card to the couple and tell them how happy you were to have gotten the opportunity to attend their wedding. Don't forget to compliment the food, the décor, the cake, and other aspects of the wedding you were impressed with.

Despite all the brouhaha over Japanese wedding etiquette, no one will really fault you for an error you make unwittingly or out of ignorance. As with everything else, it makes sense to speak to your Japanese friends and make sure you got most of the elements right about the wedding etiquette rules. Other than that, if you behave well and politely and don't get overly drunk or behave irrationally, Japanese weddings are fun and you can join the party too.

Chapter 17: Gesture and Body Language Etiquette

Talking to a Japanese person can be quite a challenge at times because they believe in speaking in short yet meaningful sentences. Moreover, silence is an accepted part of their conversations unlike in the West where silence is considered boring or even rude when two or more people are engaged in conversation.

This attitude of lots of silence and few words will be even more pronounced if you have not yet built a good rapport with the person you are talking to. In such a scenario, understanding their gestures and body language will go a long way in helping you have a meaningful conversation with someone from Japan.

Eye Contact

In Japanese culture, making eye contact for a very long time is considered rude. It is best to make eye contact for the time it takes for the individual to realize you are talking to him or her and then, maintain appropriate eye level, usually at the person's neck.

Gestures

Here is a list of fairly unique gestures used by the Japanese when talking. Many of them are not very common in the western world.

Anger – Making horns by placing both the index fingers pointing upwards with the fists touching the area near the temple

Asking for a favor or forgiveness or thanking

Clapping your hands one time in front of your face

Embarrassed or awkward

Placing an open palm at the back of the head

Calling someone forward or the beckoning gesture

This is a really unique gesture in Japan. If someone is calling you to approach them then this is what you must look for: The person's right palm will be facing down and the fingers will be out front. Then, the fingers will be dragged to the inside of the palm and then they will be flicked forward. The forward flick will be more prominent and to the novice, it will look like you are being shooed away. Please note carefully and when they repeat the gesture, you will see the fingers moving toward the palm gesturing to you to come forward.

Counting in Japan

Counting on the fingers happens in the direction that is quite opposite to what is done in the west. To start with, the entire palm and the fingers are kept open and outstretched with fingers separated from each other. When you count one, the thumb is folded into the palm. For 2, the index finger is folded over the thumb, and so forth until when you reach 5, the little finger is folded in and a fist is formed. The number of fingers that are folded in is the count and not the fingers that are open.

Saying no indirectly

The Japanese word for 'no' is '*iie*' and it is very rare for them to use this expression directly even if they actually mean it. For the Japanese culture, saying a direct no is considered rude and clumsy and, therefore, they use body language to replace the spoken *iie*. The gesture of saying no through body language is by using the embarrassment or awkward gesture along with a sharp inhalation of breath. You must look out for this 'no' gesture and learn to understand that your request is being denied.

While some of the young people in Japan have learned to say 'no' directly especially to the foreign expats there, there are many more people here who still use the gesture instead. The look of regret on the face along with the sharp intake of breath will be the clincher when they are a gesturing the 'no' signal.

Giving Directions

As it is considered rude to point fingers in Japan, when you are asked for directions, you must hold out your hand in a graceful manner and move it toward the direction you intend to show. The gesture is more like an offering (looks like a waiter with his palms out and carrying a tray) than giving directions. Watch how a Japanese colleague does it with grace and learn to repeat it.

Referring to themselves

You will see how many Japanese people during the course of a conversation are touching the tips of their noses with their index finger. This gesture means they are referring to themselves. They could be telling you their preferences about food choices or anything else. You must combine the words with this gesture and understand that they are talking about themselves.

Goodbyes and Hello Greetings

No hugging, kissing, or any public display of emotion or affection is allowed. So, the gesture to greet someone when meeting them or to say bye goes something like this: with elbows tucked into their hips and open palms facing outward near their faces, they will do a to and fro wave.

A bow is also used for the greeting. The lower and longer the bow, the more respect it conveys. Women keep their hands on their knees while bowing while the men keep their hands to their sides. Even during a telephone conversation, you will see many of the Japanese people bowing even though the other person cannot see it. Perhaps, the respect is flowing from the bow to the words!

If you notice, many of the body language cues are quite different from what is practiced in the West. Yet, most of them are sensible if you understand the idea behind the gesture and the core principle of the Japanese culture.

Chapter 18:
Japanese Festival Culture

The traditional Japanese festivals are called Matsuri and each of them has a rich history going back hundreds of years. Even today, these festivals are enjoyable, energetic, exciting, and fun to participate in. Anyone is allowed to join in the festivities. Each community celebrates the Matsuris at different times of the year.

Usually, each community's festivals are sponsored by the community shrine and organized the local people. People come dressed in the traditional Matsuri costume. The mikoshi, a heavy portable shrine, is carried through the streets of the community so that the people can be blessed.

Gion Matsuri (in Kyoto)

This is one of the most famous Matsuris in Japan and occurs throughout the month of July. It is the festival dedicated to the Yakasha shrine and dates back to 869 A.D. The highlight of the Gion Matsuri is the grand procession of different floats referred to as *Yamaboko Junko* that takes place on the 17th and the 24th of July each year on the Oike and Kawaramachi Streets. This grand procession is truly spectacular to watch.

Awa Odori (in Tokushima)

This is a dance festival in Japan and the largest one in the country. Men, women, and children all participate in the street dance which takes place in nearly all the streets of the Tokushima city. The festival takes place between 12th August and 15th August. Dressed in straw hats and summer cotton kimonos, nearly a million people turn out for this massive event. Anyone can join in the dance.

Kanda Matsuri (in Tokyo)

This famous festival in Tokyo is sponsored by the Kanda Myojin Shrine. Many portable shrines are carried through the streets of Tokyo starting from the main shrine in the morning and returning to it in the evening. Thousands of people walk with each portable shrine as it makes its way through the streets of the city showering its blessings on the onlookers and the citizens. The Kanda Matsuri parade takes place around the middle of May and covers the Kanda, Akihabara, and Nihonbashi districts of Tokyo.

Yuki Matsuri or the Snow Festival (in Sapporo)

This snow festival has its origins in 1950 when six snow statues were built by high school children in Sapporo. Since then, the Snow Festival takes place every year in February. Today, it has become an international snow sculpture contest with gigantic sculptures built that amaze the visitors and locals alike.

Nebuta Matsuri (in Aomori)

Lantern floats are the symbols of the Nebuta Matsuri, which occurs in the city of Aomori between 2nd August and 7th August every year. The lantern floats depict many human figures, and they are accompanied by thousands of dancers who also chant right through the parade. The Nebuta Matsuri parade sets off in the evening after sunset and continues for many hours.

Kishiwada Danjiri Matsuri (in Osaka)

Danjiris are heavy wooden floats (some of them weigh as much as 3000 kg). This festival takes place in the middle of September in Kishiwada City, Osaka. It is a thrilling experience to participate in this festival as you see people pulling these heavy floats at amazing speeds even as the leaders of each float hop and dance on the rooftops of these floats.

Tenjin Matsuri (in Osaka)

Supported and sponsored by the Tenmangu Shrine, Osaka, the Tenjin Matsuri takes place on the 24th and 25th of July every year. The festival is conducted to honor Sugawara Michizane, the main deity of the Tenmangu Shrine. On the second day of the festival, there are land processions and river processions. The river procession in the evening is spectacular as the lights on the floats are reflected in the water even as beautiful tapestries of fireworks light up the night sky.

Kochi Yosakoi Matsuri (in Kochi)

This festival started in 1954, as the local people added a dance flavor to it by creating the Yosakoi Naruko Dance. The special dance is based on an old folk song known as Yosakoi Bushi. Replete with up-tempo music, the people and all participants dance passionately gyrating their hips and using large clappers called Naruko. Taking place in the middle of August, the click-clack sound of the clappers reverberates through the streets of Kochi long after the festival is over.

Tanabata Matsuri (in Sendai, Miyagi)

Centered in the Sendai city of Miyagi, the Tanabata Matsuri takes place between the 6th and the 8th of August every year. This festival is dedicated to a Chinese legend about two stars named Vega and Altair and, therefore, is also called as the Star

Festival. During the festival, plenty of colorful paper decorations are used to decorate the streets of Sendai.

Hakata Dontaku Matsuri (in Fukuoka)

People dance and parade the streets of Fukuoka holding the 'shamoji,' a wooden utensil for serving rice during the Hakata Dontaku Matsuri. Also referred to as Hakata Dontaku Port Festival, during this time a lot of events and festivities take place around the Port of Hakata. The origins of this festival can be traced back to 1179 when the locals used this time to thank their lords for their generosity and kindness.

****

Can you help us?

If you enjoyed this book, then we really appreciate if you can post a short review on Amazon. We read all the reviews and your feedbacks will help us improve our future books.

If you want to leave a private feedback, please email your feedback to: feedback@dingopublishing.com

****

Conclusion

This book has been written to give you some basic insights into the rich and beautifully woven tapestry of the Japanese culture. The more you learn about it, the more you will appreciate the deep level of mindfulness that is applied by the Japanese people in the way they lead their lives.

While many of their rules of etiquette might come across as difficult-to-fathom, especially for Westerners, as you delve deep you will realize and appreciate the layers of subtleties involved in every aspect of the Japanese life, whether at the personal or professional level.

Their colorful kimonos, their deep respect for their age-old customs and rituals that they endeavor to keep alive even in the modern times, their ability to mix, mingle, and respect other cultures equally, and their rather serious outlook to life gives you new perspectives of this world that were hitherto absent in your own life.

The detailed attitude given by the Japanese people to every subtle layer of social and family life is the highlight of their culture. They refuse to take any aspect lightly and give equal importance to everything; from the seemingly mundane element of eating together or drinking tea to high levels of commercial success in their professional business.

As you live, dine and walk with your Japanese friends, you will discover new elements of life that were always there but missing to you because you have not really bothered to take in each detail. This ability to live mindfully is something that

Japanese etiquette rules teach us that will last us for a lifetime and make us more productive and happier than before.

www.DingoPublishing.com

Bonus

As a way of saying thanks for your purchase, we're offering a special gift that's exclusive to my readers.

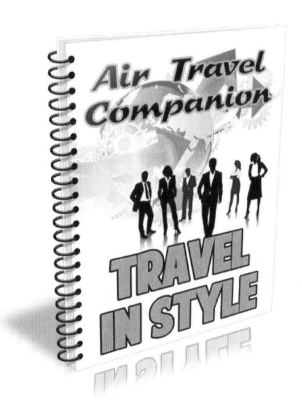

Visit this link below to claim your bonus.

http://dingopublishing.com/bonus/

More books from us

Bushido: The Samurai Code of Honour

Link: http://dingopublishing.com/book/bushido/

The Samurai were highly-skilled warriors, fighting for various reasons, even establishing the feudal era known as Edo, with a social caste system that put them on the top. The Samurai ruled Japan for several years, fought wars for 700, and eventually became obsolete.

But, their traditions and codes are not gone from history. They live on today. Everyone can learn a little something from the Samurai, including how to live a better life. Honoring people, staying loyal, and defending others when it is right are all virtues of the Samurai that can be continued today.

You are going to learn of the eight virtues, the history of the Samurai, some of the most famous warriors, and then you will discover how you can apply their lifestyle to the modern world. Wouldn't it be nice if people returned to a more chivalrous nature, where lying and devious acts are not acceptable? Where being honest, sincere, and courageous are looked upon with reverence?

The Code of the Samurai or Bushido as written by Inazo Nitobe can teach us a lot about living a decent and kind life. Discover how you can uphold the traditions of highly-skilled warriors, even if you are just a regular person.

(Book excerpt is available on page 111)

Ramen: Noodles Cookbook

http://dingopublishing.com/book/ramen-noodles-cookbook/

Ramen noodles are a staple food for numerous families, especially for those families living on a budget. These noodles are also a staple in a number of cities since they are versatile and easy to cook. This book contains the simplest and the most delicious recipes that will help you make your meals interesting and crunchy.

The noodle recipes in this book are spicy, sour and sweet. A number of recipes in the book can be prepared in a few minutes, which is an added bonus when one needs to prepare a quick meal. Ramen noodles are easy to make, so easy that children can make them too! You can tweak the recipes to make them more interesting to you. There are times when you will make your very own delicious ramen recipe, one you can share with the world.

This book contains recipes for a number of different meals. If you are in need to prepare an easy, cost-effective and quick meal, this recipe book is for you.

Book Excerpt: Bushido

Introduction

Inazo Nitobe best describes the code of the Samurai. With flowery language and a scholarly viewpoint that is the epitome of gentlemen educators, Nitobe has given the modern world an answer to what it means to examine the Samurai, the Bushido, and apply this to the contemporary world.

A phrase commonly stated today is, "Chivalry is dead." Anytime a man opens a door and does not hold it for a lady or whenever he does not get out and open the car door first. When a man forgets to use manners in front of a woman, "chivalry is dead."

For some scholars, it never existed. However, for Nitobe, the code of the Samurai was genuine, and it managed to live on well after the Western world let go of the feudal system.

Bu-shi-do translates into English as "Military-Knight-Ways," though not a very elegant translation, chivalry is considered "horsemanship," which also does not lend itself to the power of such codes people lived by.

Bushido is a "code of moral principles" which men are supposed to follow either through instruction or requirement. It is not something that is "written" but is instead a belief handed down orally throughout the feudal times. Yes, some attempted to write it, but how can one describe what is unwritten and unuttered in most circles? The heart is where the Bushido code lives on, with more than one brain or single person giving life to the ethics one should follow.

This code gave rise to the Samurai, a professional class of warriors strong enough to survive battles, start families, and gain significant honor. The Bu-ke or Bu-shi were fighting knights, with Samurai rising to high ranks of privilege and honor, taking on enormous responsibility. It was necessary for these men to have a standard of behavior to separate themselves from the "brutes" written about as nothing more than savages by the English. It was necessary for the Samurai to have a final judgment on any misdeeds to hold the rude behaviors of lesser people in check who were not worthy of being in the same ranks.

People living beyond the Samurai during Feudal Japan meant having to protect their way of life from invading forces, and certain aspects of the code still exist. These morals are seen in the customs of Japanese people, how they act towards others and work to support their families.

Having military personnel is still necessary today, and perhaps we can see the Samurai live on in the teachings they gain. After all, the Samurai and Bushido code existed to ensure Japan was safe. It stands to reason that this history of military prowess lives on in the military, as it does in other aspects of regular life.

Discover what Bushido and the Samurai Code of Honor are really about. Find the correlations that can apply to your life and the world you live in. Perhaps, you will see there are great lessons to be gained.

Chapter 1: History of the Samurai

The Samurai may have been warriors of premodern Japan, but their legacy lives on in the Bushido code. These men rose high in military ranking and eventually became the highest-ranking class. The Edo period, between 1603 and 1867, was the best era for the bushi. These great warriors were able to wield bows, arrows, spears, and guns. However, they were most known for their swords and this is what continues to symbolize their heritage.

To understand the code, or the way, of the warrior, you need to know that many of the men in the military followed Confucian teachings and Zen Buddhism. Both schools of thought are what taught the men to be respectful, have self-discipline, and that loyalty and ethical behavior were a must.

Depending on which scholar you ask, the warriors of Japan did not begin their existence until the Heian period (794-1185). A battle between different lineages of Japanese, like the Emishi people in Tohoku, showed a need for men with fighting skills.

Wealthy landowners also needed protection against armies. These owners were independent of the central government but were allowed to build armies. The two most powerful clans were Taira and Minamoto. They also created their armies to rise against the government and each other.

One of the more recognizable figures in history is Minamoto Yoritomo from the Minamoto clan. He was victorious over the government and established a new one in 1192, based on military laws. The military government was led by a supreme military commander, called a shogun. his battle helped the Samurai rule Japan for close to 700 years.

These 700 years are where many of the films by Akira Kurosawa (maybe give some context as to who he is) have come from, depicting the code of the Samurai and ninja warriors.

The period between the 15th and 16th centuries was the most chaotic, with many warring states fighting to have supremacy over others. Japan was broken into states or prefectures with distinct differences in ruling styles and laws, but one thing within these styles was common—warriors of high skills. Whether the warriors became Samurai or ninjas, it was a time when different skills evolved giving rise to the fictional depictions we know today.

At the tail end of the 15th century, Japan became united again with a social caste system, which was an unbending system that put the Samurai at the top, with farmers, artisans, and merchants below them. The shogun made the Samurai live in the castle towns, carrying the only swords. The ruling shogun decided that no one, other than warriors, could have swords, and raids occurred to remove all weapons from farmers and people below them in rank.

Samurai earned rice from their feudal lords or daimyo. Not all Samurai had masters, though. Some, known as *ronin*, left the ranks, and wandered the country, sometimes causing minor troubles in the 1600s.

The power of the Samurai was well known which allowed peace to prevail against more massive wars during the Edo period. Unfortunately, martial arts skills declined due to a lack of need, and many Samurais started taking other jobs in the government, becoming teachers or artists. By 1868, the feudal era ended and soon after, the need for the Samurai class disappeared and with it the abolishment of their caste.

Origins of the Samurai

Scholars have traced the origins of the Samurai to the Kanto plain, although not all of the men came from this area, the original warriors did. The Kanto plain is in the south of Japan, and these men worked on their skills to fight the Emishi. At first, the Samurai was considered nothing special, other than their qualifications they worked on. They were rowdy, even barbarian-like, but it was realized a code was necessary to bring up their reputation and increase their status amongst their peers and masters.

Bravery on the battlefield is one element of the Samurai that increased in prowess throughout history. Their traditions of battle cries and challenging single enemies to combat showed that these men were fearless and filled with honor.

There are different levels in the Samurai system. The gokenin or housemen was the lowest rank and the vassals of feudal lords. Goshi were rustic warriors who could farm their land, but until they reached full Samurai rank, they could not own swords. The Hatamoto or bannermen were the highest-ranking members capable of holding swords, being a part of the government, and owning land.

Despite the prowess and eventual rise to top the caste system in Feudal Japan, the Samurai made up only six percent of the population. Part of holding such a high rank meant they could kill anyone without legal repercussions, but their code also instilled certain virtues that ensured they did so only when they were in the right.

Samurai also had assistants known as baishin. These assistants worked the land for their masters. When war needed the men away from home, the baishin would take care of the property. But, with the rules about lower ranking men not being allowed to carry swords, the areas were left defenseless when Samurai were gone. few Samurai were left behind to defend the territory.

In some instances, the women were able to defend their masters' lands. A small group of female warriors did exist, but they were called onna bugeisha and were not Samurai. The words translate as martially-skilled women.

Samurai Dress and Weapons

Samurai were horse owners. They would ride into battle on horses, fighting with bows and arrows to take out as many enemies from a distance as possible. Their swords were long with a curved blade. By the 1500s,they also carried shorter swords. Hideyoshi decreed that they needed this second shorter sword. However, Only the full Samurai who could hold the two swords.

Samurai preferred to attack at night as a way of surprising the enemy.

For their dress, they wore silk cloaks called horo, which would fasten at the neck and the waist. The armor was leather and light to make it easier to move. The armor found in most museums outside of Japan came from later periods, usually the 17th century. The armor pieces were more substantial in the 1700s than in earlier centuries.

The Japanese sword is known as the katana. It is a curved sword with a blade of 60 centimeters. The blade was single edged with a slender metal. It also had a circular or square guard between the handle. The grip accommodated two hands. There is also the tachi, which was more curved than the katana, was used by earlier Samurai. . The tachi was worn with the cutting edge down, while the katana had the cutting edge up. The katana is considered one of the best in history for cutting, since it was reputed to cut steel in half. Of course, it could not, but a piece of silk falling from a short height could be cut in half.

When it comes to the sword names of Japan, the Jokoto was first, being used until 900 CE. The Koto came next as the sword of choice, until 1596. The Shinto was used from 1596 to 1780. Newer swords were the Shinshinto, Gendaito, and Shinsakuto. The Shinsakuto are made today. he katana was a word to describe the long sword, but the different names like Shinto were also used depending on the time period. Samurai had katana blades for most of their battles, using shorter swords for seppuku and closer combat. The sword was carried as a sign of honor, but not all men would use them. The skill of the Samurai would depend on what weapon he chose to wield.

Seppuku

Anyone who has seen a Samurai movie understands the word seppuku, but was it a real concept? Yes, it is true that the Samurai was expected to fight to his death if necessary. To prevent capture, a Samurai could kill himself. It was an honor to perform seppuku rather than to be executed by an enemy after being captured. Seppuku was a form of self-disembowelment. The Samurai believed the spirit was contained in the stomach area and not the heart. The ritual required the Samurai to wear a white robe, for purity, cut his abdomen with a knife from left to right. Once the cut in the stomach occurred, there was an assistant that would decapitate the Samurai. The Kaishakunin was a special sword for this purpose. Bleeding to death by a cut to the abdomen was slow and painful, thus the reason for the assistant, to decapitate as hasten the death. Retainers of the Samurai would then have to commit suicide because of their master's death. It was a code called junshi or death by following.

Several Samurais make up the legends and myths of Japan. Many of the people in these legends were real, but have been mythologized.

Bushido: The Samurai Code of Honour

Find out more at:

http://dingopublishing.com/book/bushido/

Thanks again for purchasing this book.

We hope you enjoy it

Don't forget to claim your free bonus:

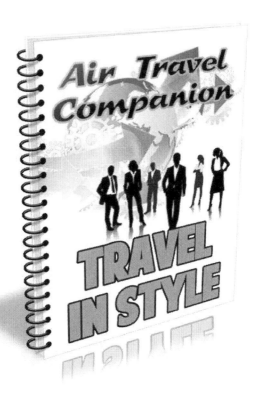

Visit this link below to claim your bonus now:

http://dingopublishing.com/bonus/